Hidden Treasure Poetry

Words of Hope, Healing, and Celebration

Porshai S. Campbell

Watersprings
PUBLISHING

Published by Watersprings Publishing, a division of

Watersprings Media House, LLC.

P.O. Box 1284

Olive Branch, MS 38654

www.waterspringsmedia.com

Contact publisher for bulk orders and permission requests.

Library of Congress Control Number: 2021901759

ISBN-13: 978-1-948877-61-9

Printed in the United States of America.

Table of Contents

Hidden Treasure Poetry

Words of Hope, Healing, and Celebration

Porshai S. Campbell

Acknowledgments

Thank you to my loving Father Jesus Christ that crowns me with His loving kindness and tender mercies. Thank You for choosing me to speak a word in due season to Your people. Gracias Dios por todas las bendiciones dulces que me brinda cada día.

To Ashira, who always encourages me to "Keep writing."

To my Mother, whose invaluable words, "Writing is your gift" guides my sails.

Thank you to my family, friends, church family, and Facebook community that continue to support my childhood writing passion with your unyielding support. You all are kindly appreciated.

Introduction

Every choice that you have made and will make, God is using to work together for your very good.

Hidden Treasure Poetry is written from the angle of women observing their lives and the beauty God has placed in their hearts to share with the world.

Then our mouth was filled with laughter,
And our tongue with singing. Then they said
among the nations, "The LORD has done great
things for them." The Lord has done great
things for us, whereof we are glad.
Psalm 126:2-3 KJV

PART I

Hope

Woman in the Room

A Black woman.
Yes, a Black woman is who I am, and a Black woman I will forever be.
For when I walk into a room you can't help but
become mesmerized with me.
"Her skin is so beautiful, they gasp, soft like
the skin of a newborn baby."
"But not one quarter has been spent engulfed in a mirror
applying synthetic facial beauty powder."

"Her hair," they whisper in astonishment under their breath, "it's so stunning, can
we touch it?" they ask.
"Most certainly," I assertively respond.
Without hesitation their white fingers rake through
each strand and they are unearthed by startling flashbacks of the hair their
ancestors cradled while nursing at their African nannies' supple breasts.
I coyishly smile and thank them for their most gracious compliments.
Each pearl in my mouth visibly twinkles.
Teeth so white, similar to freshly fallen snow, void of wrinkles.
"Let me assure you my darling
before there was crystal infused toothpaste,
I used natural products birthed from our earth's blackened treasure chest. This is
the sought-after secret to my ivory pearls' luster."

"Her cheekbones are so high – like that of the enchanting Rocky Mountains," they

whisper. "O, these?" as I slowly bring my fingers to my face, "they were delicately crafted from my Creator and slowly chiseled until they were
perfectly symmetrical."

"For God gave me these radiant cheekbones
my darling, to remind me that He has embossed me with undefeatable greatness.
If I need encouragement, I just look peripherally and I am reminded of two
pinnacle warriors that fight for me every second, every day. These mountains
protect me during the dark times when I find it impossible to lift my head. God
gave me these mountains to show me how much of an overcomer I already am."

"Your neck is so exquisitely long and sophisticated," they exclaim as their eyes
carefully dance up and down my petite frame as I enter
my runway.
"This, my friend, is no mistake. For God supplemented me with these aesthetics to
confirm that like a giraffe whose neck is long and flexible,
I too have the best vegetation, sunlight, and aerial view."
"Nevertheless all of my needs will be met because I can always reach up and pull
down.
Have you ever seen a starving giraffe?
Doesn't it always consume unblemished whole foods?"
God gently reminds me that I have never left Eden.
"Your head, My child, has always been in the clouds.
You've been too preoccupied to appreciate the fresh dew."

As my admirers appreciate my ambrosial beauty and intoxicating charm, wind
from the Rocky Mountains encapsulates me and I am teleported into the nest of
the safety of the Lord's arms unharmed.

I Do

The joy of being a woman is no simple thrill.
The pleasure of putting on high-heeled shoes is not meant to impress slow-witted slippery eels.
The perfect dress, the right tantalizing, sweet-smelling perfume,
is entangled into the mesmerizing pursuit leading to I Do.

A beautiful woman fragranced with charm and intelligence no good man can resist. These alluring qualities are what makes him lick his lips.
The way I walk, the way my enchanting presence fills a room is not meant to be appreciated by buffoons.
"She laughs at all my jokes," he says, laying gently awake at night- smiling as bright as the glistening crescent moon.

"I want her all to myself. I want to be her only bridegroom," he whispers incessantly cantering back on his stallion to his million-dollar mansion.
"She will be my wife. Even with the world's total diamond harvest and Africa's unparalleled exotic honey production, I am still weak and poor without her as my companion."

"My love, my beloved princess, little does she know she will forever be in my presence. "Her worries of how she will feed her children will never plague her spirit again. Her thoughts of not being appreciated will quickly grow dim."
"What do you see in this woman?"
Irritating inquiries of kin vex my daydreaming.

"Ah, that is something you will never understand.
For when I look into her eyes, I see the enchanting layers of the illustrious
Pacific Ocean. I see the brightest, most charming seashell twinkling on Maui's
breathtaking ivory sandy beach."
"I see one queen among several worker bees.
I see the finest and strongest plant in a British cottage, I see my hidden treasure in
a million-year-old cave."

She was once overlooked, abused, and mistreated,
but from this day forward she will be everything I have always needed.
She will know that she is my sunlight every day.
Far beyond the days when her hair starts to grey.
She will never have to cry about misfortune again because God has blessed her
to be my portion. She has waited a very long time, but as a collector of precious
jewels, my wife, my heart, my soulmate is by far the most precious gem I have
discovered.

Intentionally locking eyes with his princess, he says,
"Above all, I have searched for you all my life,
Antigua my Black American beauty.
Instead of tears you will have unforgettable years.
Sadness, confusion, anxiety, and loneliness.

Don't concern yourself with patching up these holes."
Do not remember the things of old.
I have irrevocably replaced your scars with my
Immutable love.
Impenetrable protection.
Jumping joy.

Tender touch.
Lifelong laughter.
Beautiful blessings.
Distinct destiny.
Fortress fortitude and eloquent elevation.
I love YOU and will not rest until you own my
last name and carry on my legacy.

Getting down on one knee he says,
"Will you marry me and make me the most blessed and satiated man alive?"
Slowly, wiping the gushing tears off her face, smiling ear to ear she looks up and
says, "I already said I do in my dreams now I get to say it awake-
Yes, Yes, Forever Yes, I do!"

Your Child From His Child

For unto us a Child is born.
Through one child you can exhale with confidence knowing that He always has and always will win until the very end.
Your child, the little girl you hold, has come from a Child that became a Man whose mission was to deliver people from their sins.
You name her a beautiful name.
A name significant to the ideal life you pray she will claim.

A life full of countless wins and minuscule disappointments.
Her suffocating morning hugs to the wild dandelions she picks.
To the homemade birthday cards that serve as an elixir when you become feverishly sick.
She's so precious and dependent on your love.
Even when you've burned dinner and had a bad hair day, she understands you are enough.
Her laughter is more precious than an exquisite foreign orchestra.
There isn't anyone on this planet that can replicate her gut-stitching sense of humor.

You pray she will always be strong, trust God and never take off her crown. As time passes you surprisingly discover she only briefly took off her crown to pass it down to her flawless bundle of joy with cheeks so round.

Your daughter must know she is beautiful,

irreplaceable, loved, chosen, and perfect.
Even when the world is crushing her shoulders, she must know she is an
indispensable overcomer.
Your daughter is worth more than ten sons.
Her value is priceless.
Take it from Boaz, he married a woman that never was ruthless.

Teach your daughter to speak the King's English.
To fill her palace with laughter,
and teach all souls she encounters the right praying posture.

Countless full moons and twelve-month orbits occur after her father cuts her
umbilical cord. No matter the many milestones she reaches or unforeseen
destinations, she will always be your special inheritance.
Your special delivery sent first class from heaven's radiant presence.

Whole with the Carpenter

What you see is not what you see.
I step out of the house looking more polished
each time you see me.
For I don't have to beg or plead for anything I need.
Simply because I am the daughter of the Most-High King.

You always look so nice, so classy and well-put-together they say.
Little do they know I am walking on my Lord's inflated grace.

You see, I haven't always looked so elegant, so prim and proper.
I used to have a reason as to why I had next to nothing to offer.
I would hardly put myself first or take time to appreciate the magnetic glow before
my face.
I compared myself to others and when people saw the hurt in my eyes, I slowly
looked away with shame.

But once Jesus stepped into my life, He gave
me the confidence and courage to start over again.
He says to each and every one of His creatures,
You are a blessed child of God.
You are royalty.
You are my treasure.
You have an enchanting destiny.
You have more value than any and every ancient pearl.
For I have called you.

I have taken you as my own.
When you start to feel alone look upward for
encouragement from your first home.

Apologize for your wrongdoings.
Make peace with fellowmen.
But not for one moment should you doubt
your pristine purpose.
Listen to how I see you.
"As a cloud in the sky changes, as the day turns
into night—this is how I look at you."
"Look Mommy, look at that cloud! It looks like
a despondent old man with his head bowed
down."
"No, daughter, that is a new king holding his
glistening decadent crown."
"For you are my artwork, haven't you accepted
I am the potter and you are my clay?"
"The world may see you one way
but my craftsmanship has made you okay."

"Remember I am the greatest artist, I make
everything beautiful in its own time."
Take note of the caterpillars, tadpoles,
and ladybugs unique in their own way.
These creatures started out as what the world would
view grotesque and unlovable, but after an
irrevocable transmutation they became something beautiful, people voyaged
thousands of miles to learn more about.

You are precious.
You are fearfully and wonderfully made.
You are of more value than My bite-size fluttering sparrows and crystals in a
thousand-year-old cave.
Everything in this world was made for Me to appreciate.
But you Dear One, I formed from dust particles and made every dark part of you
to illuminate.

Don't you trust My Word that states darkness
and light cannot co-exist?
Feel special, for when I was making you, I was
in pure bliss.
Focus on your internal beauty in order to stay transformed by My Word.
Just like the cloud that is construed as several different things.
It doesn't worry itself with how it's perceived or what others do or do not see.
It just relishes in its position and allows the Son to shine
Through it to become everything it's supposed to be.

Precious Promises – Hope

Psalm 139:14 KJV
I am fearfully and wonderfully made.

Isaiah 61:3 NKJV
To give unto them beauty for ashes, the oil of joy for mourning. The garment of praise for the spirit of heaviness.

Psalms 30:11 KJV
Thou hast turned my mourning into dancing.

Samuel 2:8 Berean Study Bible
He lifts me out of the dust and places me in the presence of princes.

Psalm 32:7 Berean Study Bible
You are my hiding place. You protect me from trouble. You surround me with songs of deliverance.

Psalm 84:11 KJV
For the Lord God is a sun and shield: the Lord will give grace and glory: no good thing will He withhold from them that walk uprightly.

Proverbs 18:22 KJV
He who finds a wife finds a good thing and obtains favor from the Lord.

Esther 2:17 KJV
And the king loved Esther more than the other women.

Proverbs 12:4 KJV
A virtuous woman is a crown to her husband.

Psalm 128:3 KJV
Thy wife shall be as a fruitful vine by the sides of thine house: thy children like olive plants round about thy table.

Isaiah 26:7 NIV
But for those who are righteous, the way is not steep and rough. You are a God who does what is right, and you smooth out the path ahead of them.

Psalm 22:31 NIV
They will proclaim his righteousness, declaring to a people yet unborn: He has done it.

Isaiah 54:13 NKJV
All your children shall be taught by the LORD, And great shall be the peace of your children.

Psalm 144:12 KJV
Your daughter will be like a cornerstone polished after the similitude of a palace.

Proverbs 22:1 KJV
A good name is rather to be chosen than great riches, and loving favor rather than silver and gold.

Philippians 1:3 KJV
I thank my God every time I remember you.

Philippians 4:19 NKJV
And my God shall supply all your need according to his riches and glory by Jesus Christ.

Habakkuk 3:19 KJV
The LORD God is my strength, and he will make my feet like hinds' feet, and he will make me to walk upon mine high places. To the chief singer on my stringed instruments.

Isaiah 60:11 KJV
Your gates will always stand open, they will never be shut, day or night.

Psalm 37: 4 KJV
Delight yourself in the Lord and He will give you the desires of your heart.

Daniel 2:21 KJV
He changes times and seasons; he removes kings and sets up kings; he gives wisdom to the wise and knowledge to those who have understanding.

Psalm 118:9 KJV
For it is better to put your trust in the Lord than in princes.

Proverbs 21:1 GNT
The Lord controls the mind of a king as easily as he directs the course of a stream.

Psalm 68:6 NIV
He sets the lonely in families.

PART II

Healing

Decade Joking Around

Toot your own horn in your 20's
Thrive at 30
Be fruitful at 40
Fear nothing at 50
Say it ain't so 60
70 is your season
Ain't He good at 80
90 looks nice on you
Keep it 100 at 100

Thanksgiving Praise

Lord, what do I have to be grateful for?
I don't live in a palace with servants waiting on me hand and foot.
You're right my child, but I have given you every one of My commands.
My car starts when it wants to, and the air conditioning hardly works.
The times you have suffered,
I always kept your lights on, and your heater never broke.

Okay, Lord, but what about my parents?
They weren't on the cover of Raise Your Children
Right magazine.
You have a valid point My child,
but I gifted them to raise a handsome king and prosperous queen.

Alright, you got me there Lord,
but why did I grow up alone and felt that people pushed me aside?
Every time your teacher praised you for performing well,
and your coach gave you high fives,
that was Me causing your
pain to divide.
Why did kids tease me and exclude me from their lunch tables?
It was during this time,
that I was preparing you for the special day to show
you "I am able."

My family is not Christian,
and they believe You are a figment of my wild imagination.
Yes, my dear child,
This lifelong tailored test is to make your days long and prosperous and a personal
invitation to enter My Sabbath rest.

Tell me Lord, why throughout my life has it been so hard to maintain
three close friendships?
I haven't forgotten about you. I am preparing sweeter than honey friends that
will love you and stay loyal to you until the very end.

My children, Lord, they fuss and they fight,
and I've worked so hard to supply their need;
but they only intermittently tell me they love me.
Don't stop praying for them, My child.
For they will come together to defeat the
enemy.

My life has never been picture-perfect and that is the truth.
Would you be surprised to know that
there are dozens that wish they could be just like you?
Me, Lord
Yes, you, dear one.
Instead of complaining just lay everything down at the altar.

PORSHAI S. CAMPBELL

I'm sorry Lord I had so many complaints and regrets.
Don't apologize My child, just continue filling yourself with My delicate treasure.
Every word in My book was written just for you.
Take My hand and you will never stumble or falter.
Hallelujah! Thank You Jesus- You are the best!
May I never doubt You again when You put me through divine tests.

Celestial Touch

One-touch from God is all that you need.
One decision to trust God hears your plea.
You will go from patching up holes in your blue jean pockets, to hammering holes
in your living room walls to hang your million-dollar profit.
Feeling ill to being healed.
Sad to set free.
Discouraged to encouraged.
Homeless to homeowner.
Afraid- to having freedom.
Slacking and lacking to thriving and striving.
Being on welfare to being a shareholder.
Buying groceries on food stamps to a
pampered self-employed kept queen.

Overlooked, to the woman girls look up to.
Forgotten- to serenaded by your handsome king
Timid to telling it like it is uncensored.
From fighting bullies to taking no one's bull.
From shy to a shimmering star.
Head bowed down to head held high with I am His pride.

Not making the baseball team, to savoring exquisite cuisine.
From yearning to travel outside of America.
To owning your own exotic tropical island.

To sleeping in your plush king-size bed with your doting husband
beneath the moonbeam.

Complaining about not being paid what you're worth.
To turning down countless opportunities as a result of your schedule being fully
booked.
From filling out vacation sweepstakes
to making reservations to quaint hotels flooded with celebrities avoiding the
paparazzi.
From rehashing the missed opportunity to
study abroad to living overseas in countries
you now seamlessly afford.

Praying for your husband to make his indelible entrance into your life, to deciding
which Arabian wedding gown
accentuates your bust.
From praying for more children
to producing your baby's heartbeat as million-dollar albums.
From instability to having ironclad fortress stability.
Being called the ugly duckling to modeling for Black Confidence Magazine.
Being labeled as trash to winning the Nobel Peace Prize for finding the cure to an
epidemic life-threatening rash.

From lacking parental protection,
to your friends fighting over your unparalleled
affection.
Dreading the days of saying that something
"isn't within your budget,"
to designing tailored financial budgets for opulent corporations.

From writing resumes to cashing checks made payable to you.

From waking up an hour early each day to catch public transportation to your daily grind, to catching up on your sleep after ending a morning phone conference meeting with the twenty-employee business you built from scratch.
Simply because you have been touched by the gentle hand of the K-I-N-G.

Precious Promises – Healing

Proverbs 27:9 KJV
Ointment and perfume rejoice the heart: so doth the sweetness of a man's friend by hearty counsel.

2 Corinthians 4:16 KJV
Therefore we do not lose heart. Though outwardly we are wasting away, yet inwardly we are being renewed day by day.

Proverbs 15:15 KJV
All the days of the afflicted are evil: but he that is of a merry heart hath a continual feast.

Psalm 103:5 KJV
Who satisfies thy mouth with good things so that thy youth is renewed like the eagles.

Ecclesiastes 9:11 NKJV
I returned and saw under the sun that—

The race is not to the swift, Nor the battle to the strong, Nor bread to the wise, Nor riches to men of understanding, Nor favor to men of skill; But time and chance happen to them all.

Philippians 4:19 KJV
*My God shall supply all your needs according to his
riches in glory by Jesus Christ.*

Psalm 112:1 KJV
*Praise ye the LORD. Blessed is the man that feareth the LORD, that delighteth
greatly in his commandments.*

Romans 4:17 KJV
*Even God, who quickeneth the dead, and calleth those things which be not as though
they were.*

Psalm 34:10 KJV
*The young lions do lack, and suffer hunger: but they that seek the LORD shall not
want any good thing.*

Proverbs 3:5 KJV
*Trust in the Lord with all thy heart and lean not to your own understanding. In all
thy ways acknowledge Him and He will direct thy path.*

Psalm 126:3 KJV
The LORD hath done great things for us; whereof we are glad.

Psalm 103:5 KJV
Who satisfies thy mouth with good things so that thy youth is renewed like the eagles.

Psalm 22:31 NIV
They will proclaim his righteousness, declaring to a people yet unborn: He has done it.

Psalm 144:12 KJV
Your daughter will be like a cornerstone polished after the similitude of a palace.

Proverbs 22:1 KJV
A good name is rather to be chosen than great riches, and loving favour rather than silver and gold.

Philippians 1:3 NIV
I thank my God every time I remember you.

Isaiah 66:13 NIV
As a mother comforts her child, so will I comfort you.

Isaiah 44:5 NIV
Some will proudly say I belong to the Lord.

Proverbs 31:30 KJV
Favor is deceitful, and beauty is vain: but a woman that feareth the LORD, she shall be praised.

Ecclesiastes 18:6 NIV
"Can I not do with you, Israel, as this potter does?" declares the Lord. "Like clay in the hand of the potter, so are you in my hand, Israel."

Ecclesiastes 3:11 NIV
The Lord has made everything beautiful in its own time.

Proverbs 13:12 NKJV
Hope deferred makes the heart sick, but when the desire cometh it is a tree of life.

Ecclesiastes 3:1 KJV
To everything there is a season, and a time to every purpose under heaven.

PART III

Celebration

Don't Forget Who I Am

You might feel broken but
You are Blessed.

You might hurt deep down to the core, but You have
Hope.

You may even be fearful, but God still is
Faithful.

Rejected
but the blood of the Lamb constantly
Redeems You.

Defeated in keeping your word but your Father
is Bountiful in all His promises.

Your children might be acting up
but He has Never Let You Down.

You might feel sick and exhibit sick symptoms
but by His stripes you are Healed.

You might feel unwanted, but God has

said that He has Chosen You.
People might talk bad about you
but He has said,
No Weapon Formed Against You Shall Ever
Prosper.

You might feel like you've been made a fool of
but God has Forgiven all your follies.

Ugly
but God has crafted you into His plan of
making everything beautiful in His own time.

Outcasted
but God has Drawn You Near under His
Impenetrable wings of Safety.

Defeated
but Jehovah Nissi is your Defender, Sword, and
Shield.

Overwhelmed
but Jehovah El- Shaddai has Promised to
Renew your Strength.

Overlooked, but
Yahweh El Roi Sees you and Calls You by your
Name.

Stupid but God has given you His mind to Create, Thrive, and
Accelerate.
At times you might feel worthless-like a piece
of trash.
But Jehovah Hoseenu has said that You are
His Chosen Treasure.

Guilty
but God's grace has forgiven all your iniquities,
and He has given you a Double Portion of
Honor in place of your shame.

You may not know what tomorrow brings
but Jehovah Shammah has promised to Go
before you, to Be With You and to make All
your Crooked Places Straight.

PORSHAI S. CAMPBELL

Father's Closest to God

Father's in every continent,
and in every sun-kissed place, you are all exceptional papas.
Your children do not realize they have a precious treasure.
You wake up early and go to bed late just to ensure their well-being and prosperity
is secure.
You earn so they will never have to yearn for anything.

When you are tired and worn out you muster the strength to fulfill their endless
needs.
Not only do you relentlessly care about your precious beauties, but you protect
them like a mother grizzly bear walking her cubs in one hundred degree weather.
"Thank you, Dad," may fail to slip from their lips but you never become angry.
You just keep maneuvering your faith-led ship.

Your plate of responsibilities is unspeakable,
but your children are always the main course
even when they are emotionally unreachable.
You are a man that loves your children no matter their flaws.
As God quiets you with His love, when they are wrong or hurting,
you cover them with your shawl of selfless learning.

Some people may say what they want about you as a father,
but never spend one second acknowledging their empty words.
The proof is in the pudding- you are more than a conqueror.
When you rest your head at night just remember that God is meticulously
sculpting your path and renewing your strength.
The sun will retire, and the moon will appear.
The stars that cast out darkness represent your
resilience to embrace your silent fear.

You, brave one, are an enchanting shimmering beam.
Your fluorescent glow emanates to fatherless children near and far.
Your unspoken whispers,
"Keep looking up- dream farther than Mars," imprints children's hearts coping
through unerasable domestic violence scars.

As your heavy head dozes off to sleep, remember the treasure you possess is far
deeper than the naked eye can see.

PORSHAI S. CAMPBELL

The Power of One

One God, One Love.
One baptism. One life. One Spirit.
One name that is above every name.

One breath of a newborn baby.
One breath of God to create the world.
One moon. One earth. One orbit around the sun.

One egg and one sperm to make one child.
One mother's look at her newborn baby.
One father's look at his firstborn son.

One message for one group of people sent to
one man – Moses.
One man – Belteshazzar that saw one handwriting
encrypted message.
One man to baptize Jesus – John the Baptist.
One chosen woman – Mary.
One fervent prayer of a determined woman – Hanna.
One boy that heard one voice from God – Samuel.

One man – Adam.
One woman – Eve.
One Sabbath, one rest.
One man Noah – built one ark.

One star to lead us to one Savior – Jesus
One angel – Michael
One fast to save just one more person.

One idea to create one invention.
One penny added up to make one dollar.
One captain with one destination.
One raindrop to start a thunderstorm.

One heartbeat – birth.
One obstacle.
One celebration.
One milestone.
One last heartbeat – death.

One last paper to write.
One last exam to take.
One graduation.
One spare tire.
One quarter to make one call home.
One prayer to change the world.
One spark to cause a fire.
One seed to grow a luscious forest.

One look at the bride coming down the aisle.
One proud husband that makes the best decision of his life.
One final resurrection at one unique time for humankind –
and with one Man Jesus, you have Won, Won, Won.

Precious Promises – Celebration

Job 8:7 NIV
Though you started with little you will end with much.

Zephaniah 3:17 KJV
The LORD thy God in the midst of thee is mighty; he will save, he will rejoice over thee with joy; he will rest in his love, he will joy over thee with singing.

John 15:16 KJV
Ye have not chosen me, but I have chosen you, and ordained you, that ye should go and bring forth fruit, and that your fruit should remain: that whatsoever ye shall ask of the Father in my name, he may give it to you.

Psalm 126:5 KJV
They that sow in tears shall reap in joy.

Isaiah 6:7-8 KJV
For your shame ye shall have double; and for confusion they shall rejoice in their portion: therefore in their land they shall possess the double: everlasting joy shall be unto them.

Psalm 32:8 NIV
I will instruct you and teach you in the way you should go; I will counsel you with my loving eye upon you.

Job 23:10 KJV
But he knows the way that I take: when he has tested me, I shall come forth as gold.

Psalm 147:3 NKJV
He heals the brokenhearted and binds up their wounds.

Matthew 10:30 KJV
And the very hairs on your head are all numbered.

Psalm 37:25 NIV
I am young and now I am old, yet I have never seen the righteous forsaken or their children begging for bread.

Psalm 103:4 KJV
Who redeemeth thy life from destruction; who crowneth thee with loving kindness and tender mercies.

Isaiah 37:25 NIV
The LORD makes firm the steps of the one who delights in him.

Deuteronomy 31:8 KJV
It is the LORD who goes before you. He will be with you; He will not leave you or forsake you. Do not fear or be dismayed.

1 Peter 2:9 KJV
But you are a chosen people, a royal priesthood, a holy nation, God's special possession, that you may declare the praises of him who called you out of darkness into his wonderful light.

Matthew 11:28 KJV
Come unto me, all ye that labour and are heavy laden, and I will give you rest.

Proverbs 23:22 Holman Christian Bible
Listen to your father who gave you life and do not despise your mother when she is old.

Malachi 4:6 NKJV
And he will turn the hearts of fathers to their children and the hearts of children to their fathers.

Psalm 146:9 KJV
He relieveth the fatherless and widow.

Psalm 68:5 KJV
A father of the fatherless, and a defender of the widows, is God in His holy habitation.

Surprise!!!

BONUS TREASURE!

Faith–Building Affirmations

1. I have made a firm and unwavering decision to be happy.

2. I am responsible for my own happiness.

3. I am determined to heal my brokenness by taking small steps every day by praying, journaling, seeking professional support, and being honest with myself.

4. I make wise decisions every day with God's help.

5. I love, cherish, value, and accept all the unique gifts the Lord has given me.

6. I am confident in who I am.

7. I am doing the best that I can with my resources.

8. The Lord is making me stronger and stronger each day.

9. It is okay to ask for what I want and need.

10. There is no one like me, therefore I am only in competition with myself.

Draw the dreams the Lord has put into your heart –
allow yourself to dream big, big, BIG!

Sow your seed in the morning, and in the evening let your hands not be idle, for you do not know which will succeed, whether this or that, or whether both will do equally well. **Ecclesiastes 11:6 NIV**

PORSHAI S. CAMPBELL

41